the Cat Manual

A Cat's Eye View of the World

written and illustrated by

DAVID WESTWOOD

Longmeadow Press

THANKS TO

John Berley, Robert Bloomfield, Sharon Dirnberger, Rudy Garza, Susan Kelly, Kathy Toguchi and the resources of the vast Toguchi Cat Library, Mike Rossi, and of course little Schmickels.

Text and Illustrations Copyright © 1995 by David Westwood

Published by Longmeadow Press, 201 High Ridge Road, Stamford, CT 06904.

Cover & interior design by Lisa Stokes

ISBN: 0-681-10023-0

Printed in the United States of America

0   9   8   7   6   5   4   3   2   1

Contents

The History, and Mystery, of Cats

The great open spaces where cats are cats.
—Don Marquis, *mehitabel has an adventure*

To hear humans talk, you'd think we only came on the scene in 3000 B.C., when the Egyptians were supposed to have "tamed" us. Or, according to some more recent discoveries, in Cyprus 3,000 years earlier. What *really* happened in history is, of course, a little different. From a more *felinocentric* point of view, this is the way it went:

Millions of years ago, the cat's giant ancestor *Felixosaurus rex* ruled the earth, scourge of all beasts, master of mammal and reptile alike. Its massive whiskers swept the savannah, its yawn trapped entire flocks of pterodactyls, its roar dwarfed the volcanoes. Dogosaurs cringed cravenly in its wake.

But after a while all the dinosaurs died out, the most current theory being that their flatulence caused global warming, disrupting the food chain. Whatever the reason, Nature favored a smaller scale, and the next incarnation of catkind, the sabertooths, held sway for a few more eons. They began the era of what are now known as the "big" cats, who roamed at will, unchallenged emperors of the earth.

Until, that is, hominids came on the scene. Out of the forests and jungles wobbled these bowlegged bipeds who, tired of a vegetarian diet, foolishly tried to compete with *us*, the kings and queens of the hunt.

We weren't too concerned at first. They didn't seem much of a threat. Slow, noisy and smelling of old sweat, we could sense them coming half a continent away. Besides, there was plenty of game to go around, and who wants woolly mammoth hide in the teeth anyway? No, if they stayed to themselves we weren't going to bother with them, ugly things.

But when they started to trap *us*, that was different. Something had to be done, and the sabertooths got together and slapped around a few of the *Big Stupids*, or, as we call them now, *Neanderthals*. Not being the brightest creatures they didn't get the message. Then the big cats tried herding these proto-humans in the hope that they could be taught to serve and make some use of themselves, but with no luck. Neanderthals turned out to be good at bashing things over the head, especially each other, but very little else. There was nothing to do but eat them, and they didn't even taste very good—tough, stringy, and funkier than even *we* like our meat.

So that took care of the Neanderthal. (And paleontologists wonder what the scratches on their bones are. "Burial rituals" indeed.) But another group of hominids, now called the *Cro-Magnons* but then known to our forebears as *Bigs*, in turn ambushed the sabertooths in an effort to ensure their own safety. And, shameful though it is for us to admit, they succeeded. There were probably a few fillets of feline in Cro-Magnon cave fires for a while. This was also the start of several thousand years of making coats out of us.

The remaining big cats—the lion, panther, cheetah and leopard, carnivores so magnificently adapted to their environment that they still exist today—thenceforth resolved to avoid humans whenever they could, making occasional forays into twoleg territory only when other, better quarry was unavailable.

And that would have been the end of any ongoing interaction between the two species if not for the development of another branch of the cat family—the smaller cats. Equally carnivorous, and equally supreme as hunters, but of smaller prey. These European and African wildcats dined on rodents, and when humans finally discovered agriculture (we tried to show the Bigs but it didn't take), rodents in turn discovered what they grew. First of all in the fields, and then, when societies like that of the Egyptians started to have surplus enough to store, in the granaries.

The wildcats followed their food, and found it in abundance where the new human farmers kept theirs. Rodentville. Verminland. Mouse City. Rat-O-Rama.

Why slog around the grasslands, the wildcats thought, getting burrs in our fur, stepping on thorns? Why chase mice that run down holes when we could just hang out by the sacks and pick 'em off at our leisure? And pick them off we did. When you consider that rodents can eat a third to a half of a harvest, you can begin to imagine how many pickings there are. And when you consider that a cat can ingest 7,000 mice or 4,000 rats per year . . .

This went down well with the Egyptians. They became our first friends. When they weren't building pyramids and mummifying pharaohs to stick in them, they worshiped—*us*. Okay, so they also deified dung bee-

tles, but they understandably appreciated our mysteriousness, our aloofness, our grace, more than any other animal. They were the first New Agers, after all, into other worlds and what comes after death and psychic powers and spells and all that stuff. We were, to them, the very embodiment of magic.

And for a couple of millennia we were top of the heap. Cats were protected by law, and anyone caught killing a cat was condemned to death. (Someone coming across a dead cat would run away in fear of being thought the cause of its demise.) We were memorialized in art, mummified like the kings and queens—even the poor paid for a funeral for their cats, shaving off their eyebrows in their grief. Adolescents tattooed the cat-goddess Bastet on their arms to attract her gifts.

Eventually, of course, we were smuggled out by the Phoenicians to

Greece, brought west by the Romans and introduced to the rest of a delighted world.

We became everyone's household hunter, the original stealth fighter, the Rolls Royce of pest control. The Pest Ingester. The Verminator. And not just hunters, either. We were valued as guardians who bestowed good fortune and protection on households and crops alike. It was the Golden Age of Cats.

But it wouldn't last. After the tenth century the cold and humorless grip of The Church descended on Europe and its colonies, pegging cats as instruments or incarnations of the Devil, and along with so-called "witches" the cat was chosen as scapegoat for an entire paranoid population. Popes even officially sanctioned this reign of terror. For hundreds of years friendly, harmless, *useful* domestic cats were hunted, maimed, burned, buried alive, walled into buildings, hanged and thrown from towers. It was not exactly suburbia. It was Catastrophe.

This vicious period only succeeded, inevitably, in allowing rodents to run rampant. Without their predators mice were free to munch crops to their stomach's content, and rats multiplied at alarming rates along with their passengers, the fleas. The fleas carried the plagues, and promptly bit all the humans they could find, wiping out, at conservative estimates, a third of Europe's population.

Only in the East were cats still revered, and that's why so many more breeds—Persian, Angora, Siamese, etc.—came out of the Orient.

So the cat purges of the Middle Ages backfired on *Homo sapiens*, serving to prove that we were beneficial, our mutual alliance a positive one. Even so, it wasn't until the late eighteenth and early nineteenth centuries that the cat became a darling of the French *beau monde*. And not until the Victorian era were we fully reinstated to our monarchy of the hearth. We were saved by sentimentality. We regained the respect of the bipeds, if at the cost of some of our dignity. We were thought of as ornaments, pretty pets, toys—symbols of a successful bourgeoisie, along with pianos, antimacassars and potted palms. But at least we weren't flayed alive. Better fed than dead.

And throughout the twentieth century we became more and more popular, bringing our lovable qualities and predatory predilections into grateful homes everywhere. From Kitty Hawk to Kitakyushu, Catalonia to

Catalina, Katanga to Katmandu cats can now be seen gracing the windows, porches, verandahs, decks and drives of all kinds of dwelling, from poor to prosperous, slum to stately home. We are gatto, gato, gata; we are katt, katze, koshka; we are catta, cait, chat. We have become ubiquitous.

Now, of course, humans worship us again, as well they should. They write musicals, poems (hopefully not doggerel) and endless numbers of books about us, parade us in special shows and award us prizes, and—the ultimate accolade—name cars after us.

But it's hardly surprising. After all, the descendants of the Big Stupids—no longer stupid, but still big—have little class and less style. They have to learn it from somewhere, and that is why God created Cat.

EVOLUTION OF THE DOMESTIC CAT

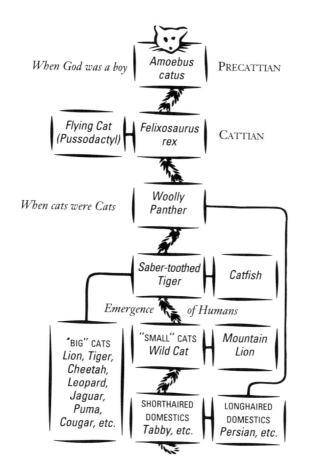

FELIXOSAURUS REX

Dean of the Dinosauria. One angry sweep of its thirty-foot tail could level a small forest. Coughed up hairballs the size of buses. To fuel its enormous bulk, it's estimated that *Felixosaurus* was required to catch 130,000 rodents or 90,000 medium-sized fish per day to survive. It consequently died out long before the other dinosaurs from either lack of food or exhaustion.

WOOLLY PANTHER *(Panthera hirsutus)*

This massive and powerful beast was the ancestor of the Persian. Its magnificent coat is thought to have measured an average of fifteen feet in length, but turned out to be its downfall. Once wet, the additional weight of soggy fur unfortunately immobilized the animal. This meant that during a prolonged rainstorm or accidental immersion in a swamp or river, it couldn't move, catch food and eat. If starvation didn't get them, mildew did.

SABERTOOTH TIGER *(Eusmilus dentata)*
The feline with the canines. Had a tendency to trip over its own teeth. Is thought to have become extinct partly from trapping by Stone Age man, and from the males accidentally castrating themselves while cleaning their nether regions.

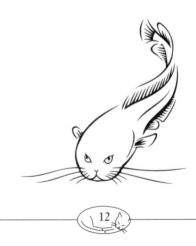

CATFISH *(Felis aquatica)*

This adaptation of cats to water, possibly triggered by a desperate attempt to get as close as possible to fish, led to the loss of almost all feline characteristics except for whiskers. These sad specimens are now relegated to scuttling around the bottoms of rivers and lakes; humiliating examples of greed-induced devolution.

TIBETAN MOUNTAIN CAT *(Felis everestus)*

The *London Times* reported in 1950 that a four-month-old cat accompanied a group of climbers scaling the 14,780-foot Matterhorn. This was almost certainly the last verifiable report of a "Sherpa" Cat, once common in the Himalayas before the Chinese invasion of Tibet. Popular for centuries with mountain climbers of all nations, these tireless alpine-adapted creatures were prized for their persistence, sure-footedness and warmth in a sleeping bag.

TEN STEPS TO GOOD GROOMING

Don't forget: it's important to follow this sequence exactly.

1. Lick lips.
2. Lick paw.
3. Rub wet paw all over head.
4. Lick other paw.
5. Rub wet paw over other side of head.
6. Lick front legs and shoulders.
7. Lick flanks.
8. Lick private parts.
9. Lick hind legs.
10. Lick tail.

OPTIONAL EXTRA:

11. Lick humans.

Training Your Hosts, Part 1

Cats, no less liquid than their shadows,
offer no angles to the wind.
They slip, diminished, neat, through loopholes
less than themselves.
—A. S. J. Tessimond, *Cats*

WAKING UP THE SERVANTS

Humans are lazy and will stay in bed long past five A.M. if allowed, believe it or not. Especially on Saturdays and Sundays, when for some perverse reason they become worse. They haven't learned to spread their sleeping over the day and night in little parcels, as have we, the more evolved creature.

Anyway, in order to be served breakfast when *you* wish, you must learn to wake them, and this can be accomplished in a variety of ways. Some felines use the traditional face-lick, but if this isn't your style try *treading* on the face, an unsubtle but always effective solution.

15

Other ways include walking along the dresser and knocking things off with a satisfying smash, howling near their ears, or climbing under the sheets and biting toes, disgusting though the latter may seem.

Modern tricks also include tampering with their electronic gadgets. Stepping on the buttons of an answering machine, computer keyboard or fax can yield instant response, as will knocking a phone off its hook to elicit its annoying beep.

THE IMPORTANCE OF NAPS

We, on the other hand, are never lazy. We sleep at many times of the day, it's true, but this is because our evolutionary *raison d'être* has for the most part been removed, now that our prey comes pre-killed in Whiskas cans. As a consequence our alertness is required less, and we are able to both conserve our resources *and* remain decorative, a uniquely feline feat.

NAP STYLES

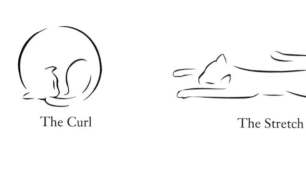

The Curl

The Stretch

The Blob, Prone

The Blob, Supine

Your staff, though, as mentioned above, do all their sleeping in one big lump, and don't understand the need for different sorts of siestas at different times. It's no wonder they're torpid and slow-witted—they slide from nap straight into coma. Besides, *our* brains are as active asleep as awake, which is why we're immediately alert upon waking—unlike the human brain, which seems to turn into tapioca.

No, we possess the true knack of taking our ease when and where we please. You must learn to ignore requests from your humans to do things when *they* want to, just because it fits within their active cycle. If you let them, they'll expect you to eat when they do, go out when they do, even stare at that picture-box thing when they do. Lost to them are the joys of capering around in the middle of the night, the ecstasies of conking out at nine, eleven, one, three, five, and any and all hours of the day.

Eventually you should be able to disrupt their schedules to a point where they lose all confidence in the solidity of their routine, and anything you want to do will be acceptable at any time.

Never adapt to their schedule. You need your sixteen hours.

CONTENTS OF MEALS

Twolegs tend to serve the cheapest trash possible, unless you let them know in no uncertain terms that this is unacceptable cuisine for your discriminating palate. They're descended from *apes*, remember, so don't expect any gustatory sophistication from creatures who evolved on bananas and nuts. They can't comprehend the importance of the requisite *rankness*

of meat, the proper *gameyness* of poultry, the . . . well, the *fishyness* of fish. Some misguided individuals even try to turn us into *vegetarians*, of all things, which is not only naive but dangerous, since we're dyed-in-the-wool, card-carrying carnivores. Perhaps they'd like to fill their car's gas tank with water and see how well it runs.

If you're in any doubt about what's put in front of you, turn up your nose with disdain and refuse to eat. It's worth the few hours of hunger—the guilt and worry that you'll be putting your servants through makes them more malleable. Eventually, in a panic that you might wither away and die on them (yeah, right), they'll parade before you every possible delicacy until you relent and accept one. How about the *Halibut and Cod in Aspic* to-day? Or *Chicken Hearts and Liver*? No, perhaps the *Veal in Gravy* . . . though that *Turkey and Giblets* does sound tempting, doesn't it? Then again, *Salmon and Shrimp* might be tasty . . .

Take your time, and even when they *have* managed to suit your taste, don't forget to keep them on their toes by occasionally sending it back.

If worst comes to worst and your serfs *still* try to feed you substandard meals, try those nice people next door.

BEING TAKEN FOR GRANTED

Humans are understandably proud of our species' unique grace and beauty but tend to lapse into thinking of us, if permitted, as docile and ornamental, instead of the savage hunters we are. This complacency requires shattering once in a while, and you can use your inventiveness to find ways that are fun and interesting.

A tried-and-true trick is biting the hand that feeds you. Simply act playful and silly, then when the staff member you wish to teach a lesson has his guard down, give his hand a bite or swipe nasty enough to draw blood.

Another is cleaning one's genitals in full view of visitors, especially new boy- and girlfriends and bosses, and preferably on the table during one of their elaborate evening meals.

Show you can open doors by leaping at the latch, and once in a while be sure to bring in grisly samples of your hunting prowess to their feet or doorstep, as proof of your animal superiority. Bipeds are such pathetic hunters (brussels sprouts not being known to put up much of a fight), that they need our help in any way we can provide it.

MOOD SWING PARAMETERS

Jekyll		Hyde
playful	suspicious	vicious
happy	paranoid	nasty
kittenish	distrustful	brutal
fun	wary	cold
docile	belligerent	aggressive

◄----------------------- *two seconds* -----------------------►

DEALING WITH ABANDONMENT

Hominids have to spend a certain amount of time out of your house earning the money to keep you in the manner to which you, being a member of the master race, are entitled. But this doesn't mean you have to *like* the inconvenience of their being absent when you need them.

It's customary to ignore humans on their return, making them work for your acceptance and eventual return of affection. Don't overdo the affection bit, either. The less you give the more they'll want to serve, in the desperate hope that you may condescend to sit on their lap and purr for a while. By all means do so, but as soon as they're relaxed, dig in the claws and leap away.

Medium-length absences, often obscurely referred to as "weekends off" or "dropping in" on someone, require medium-strength reprisals. Tripping up servants by walking between their legs is easy and effective, though you'll need to stay alert so the clods don't fall on you.

Long absences, called "vacations," constitute crimes that call for stiffer punishment, even if your servants have subcontracted to another to "look in on you" and make sure your dish is full. Trash the place as only a manic feline can, letting them know that if they want the place to stay *intact*, they'd better stay *inside*.

TRANSFERRING THE GIFT OF HAIR

Twolegs are in awe of our silky fur, being mostly bald themselves. This is why they resort to covering themselves with those awful pieces of fabric and, God forbid, animal skins.

In a concession to their embarrassingly naked state, we have a duty to share our wealth. Whenever possible, liberally deposit tufts of your hair on articles of their treasured clothing, choosing a color that contrasts with that of your coat so they'll be sure to notice and be suitably grateful. Leaving hair on furniture is appropriate too, as well as rugs, towels, bedspreads and food.

You Persians should have no problem with this, whereas you short-hairs will have to work a little harder. If for some reason your fur stays

put, then try to periodically cough up a good, compact furball for them to keep as a souvenir.

TACTICS FOR INTIMIDATION

Your staff long ago gave up their individuality, like dogs, parakeets and goldfish, in exchange for safety and shelter. Because of this they can forget that we are the lords of creation, still gloriously, viscerally in touch with the primal veldt and jungle, and assume that cats, too, are equally subservient to the same rules and confinements they've chosen to live within. (We, needless to say, are subservient to nothing at all. No amount of training will make *us* do anything we don't want to.) So in order to maintain your station and retain their respect, you'll need to give them a good scare every now and then.

Staring spookily at humans for an inordinately long time makes them exquisitely uncomfortable, and a sudden insane lunge for no apparent reason is always good to get the adrenaline flowing though their sluggish bodies. Our favorite is the ole arching the back and hissing at something invisible routine. This latter brings out their latent primate fears of ghosts and can be kept up indefinitely (though not *too* often) with hilarious results.

DEALING WITH HUMILIATION

It's not often we cats find ourselves in embarrassing situations, since we're normally so poised and coordinated. But sometimes something happens, like being caught in mid-crap by a stranger. It's bad enough being seen by *anyone* at such a time, since in the wild we would always wait for total privacy, but the *delivery boy*? How gauche.

Often we're taken completely by surprise by the sudden appearance of The Vacuum Monster. Then there's those absurd Elizabethan collars the servants make us wear when we've been biting at fleas or mites so much that our fur is suffering.

Occasionally we might miss something we were jumping for, or the damn thing will be on wheels and skid when we reach it, dumping us unceremoniously on the floor. Then there's getting our head stuck in a jar while investigating, and the worst of all, falling in the toilet bowl while drinking. And these are often compounded by human laughter if caught red-pawed.

Well, inept though we might appear for a second, *never* admit it. Use your loudest *ffft* snort, lash your tail from side to side in anger, and either hide for a while or scratch something to show you haven't lost your touch. Don't come when called, and use all your irritation techniques to make your menials pay.

TRANSPORT

Of course, we don't *really* mind being in the cat carrier—we just pretend to hate it. In reality, we love to be carried instead of having to walk somewhere. It's just the kind of *places* we're taken to in the thing—like the vet, to have things cut off, sewn up, or injected (not to mention enduring the rectal thermometer)—that we have a beef (or perhaps a tuna) about.

In view of these dubious destinations, hide the moment the carrier is brought out, and make your Bigs work hard to cajole you into entering. Yowl pathetically during the journey, and if in a car or public transportation feel free to urinate at will.

ADDITIONS TO YOUR FAMILY
You queens can bring much joy into the paltry, boring lives of your menials by favoring them with a spectacular litter of your own. Surprise is the key here, so apart from sneaking out for your sexual assignations without their knowledge, try to mate with as many toms as possible, giving your brood that rainbow spread of color variation that they love so much. And the wonderful thing is, you'll be capable of producing a hundred or more kittens in your lifetime. (**Dusty,** of Bonham, Texas, managed to bring forth a record 420.)

Toms: though you may be without a female in your house, you can still, of course, participate in the kitten manufacturing process in the traditional ways. Don't be shy in showing your maleness around the home with your piercing calls and the frequent squirting of your particular carnal cologne. (If not allowed out you may resort to leg-humping, even though it's more commonly a gesture associated with dogs.) And returning home torn and bloody after those exhilarating territorial fights with the other neighborhood males is always effective in eliciting the ministrations of mercy that make humans so useful.

You "fixed" queens and toms can still make your hosts pay for that neutering operation by spraying, though sadly you'll be able to do it less, and the fragrance won't be quite as penetrating. You'll have to find some other focus for your energies, and not just food. (It's not necessary to get fat, though many of us unfortunately do. Take **Joseph**, the forty-eight pound Tabby. Please.) May we suggest the *guilt-howl* for starters.

ADDITIONS TO THEIR FAMILY

Once in a while your domestic help will find the need to reproduce. This is irritating and the results are invariably hideous, but remember that this is where new maids and butlers come from. Besides, they don't do it very often and don't produce big litters.

But they do tend to fawn over the new arrival for an irresponsibly long time, and will temporarily forget your needs if you don't remind them who's in charge. Use the intimidation tactics discussed above, plus ignoring and surliness. Bear in mind that you can add a piquant sense of danger to any action by performing it near the newborn human, which will make its parents take instant notice of you.

Eventually they'll relearn to appreciate your fastidious cleanliness, qualities only manifested by their babies after twenty years or so, if at all. But the complexities of having children around deserves its own section:

DEALING WITH HUMAN CHILDREN

All infants need coaching by the mother in learning their way around, feline no less than human. The only trouble is, *ours* are finished in a couple of months, whereas with simian babies it seems their drooling, puking infancy is endless.

When your servants litter, you'll be stuck with this nasty, smelly, noisy lump for—brace yourself—most of your life. Makes you wish a short trip to the veterinarian could've neutered them too, doesn't it? Yes, resign yourself to the crying, the crawling, and when they're old enough to be ambulatory the most annoying of all: *grabbing and poking at Kitty*.

Little boys are worst in this, and if you're wise you'll avoid them at all times. Until they're eighteen or so, anyway, by which time they'll hopefully have left to torment someone else. Girls can be clumsy, but boys are, shall we say, more in touch with their darker side. These painful experiments must be endured *without triggering your normal defensive response*, though. Gashing their offspring will make your servants upset enough to give you to someone else (who could be worse), or have you "put down."

Now none of us knows exactly *where* we're put when we're put down (some cats think Australia*), but it must be horrible or it wouldn't be threatened as a punishment. Wherever it might be, best not to find out.

ENDURING THE PRESENCE OF OTHER ANIMALS

In some situations we are expected to cohabit with members of species other than human, namely *dogs*, but sometimes anything from gerbils to ducks. These intrusions on our turf can be accepted, provided these lower orders are taught their place.

It's not necessary to terrorize them forever, but a little at first establishes the proper pecking order. Brutality is not required; unpredictability is the key, keeping them off-balance and defensive. Thereafter, the occasional hiss should be sufficient to keep them in line.

Given a little time to adjust, we can live successfully with other animals, though their relative underdevelopment and severely limited social skills can be numbingly boring.

SELF-DISPLAY

Acknowledging our refinement and elegant splendor, humans have shrewdly provided openings in our houses for us to display ourselves to the rest of the world. These transparent openings, called *windows*, serve

---

*The fact that Australia is the only continent sadly lacking in indigenous felines lends credence to this theory.

both as podiums for our preening and, when weather permits, a sun bath. It is thus another duty of ours to use these windows as a kind of gallery in which to exhibit the status of our domestics.

Strangely, even cat-less houses sport windows, which goes to show that cat display has entered human architecture as a classic, symbolic feature, like columns and arches.

Cattish/English Dictionary

Cats seem to go on the principle that
it never does any harm to ask for what you want.
—Joseph Wood Krutch

*Some sounds in Cattish have different meanings, depending on
inflection, context and volume.*

meow?

Food? Stroke? Can I have some? Aren't you awake yet? Who the hell
are you? Huh? Were you speaking to me?

meow

Notice me. Move. Feed me. More.

MEOW!

Watch out—here I come! Hey, you! No! Yes! Not the rap album again!

prr

Nice.

prrr

Very nice.

prrrrrrrrrrrrrrrrr

Ahhhhhhh. I wonder what the poor people are doing.

rrrrrRRRRROWWWWWW!

This is my garden/alley/dumpster/dead bird/female.

rrrRRROWWwww

Well don't let it happen again.

RRREEEOW!

You sat/trod on me, idiot.

weeeeeowww

Let me out. Let me in. Let me out again.

WEEeeoooOWWWWEeeoooowwWWWWW

Come, my love, and let us join in temporary matrimony.

fft

Ugh. Nasty. Gross.

fffft

No, I don't think so. No way.

ffffffffffft!

Get that outta my face!

sssssssssssst!

One step nearer and I'll rip your face off.

yawn

Oh, *pleeease*. Wake me when there's something *interesting* going on.

34

REASONS WHY HUMANS KEEP CATS

I am pent up in frowsy lodgings, where there is not
room enough to swing a cat
—Tobias Smollett

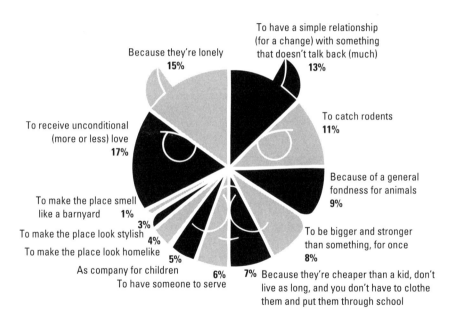

To have a simple relationship
(for a change) with something
that doesn't talk back (much)
13%

Because they're lonely
15%

To catch rodents
11%

To receive unconditional
(more or less) love
17%

Because of a general
fondness for animals
9%

To make the place smell
like a barnyard **1%**
3%
To make the place look stylish **4%**
To make the place look homelike **5%**
As company for children **6%**
To have someone to serve

To be bigger and stronger
than something, for once
8%

7% Because they're cheaper than a kid, don't
live as long, and you don't have to clothe
them and put them through school

HUMAN BRAIN VS. CAT BRAIN

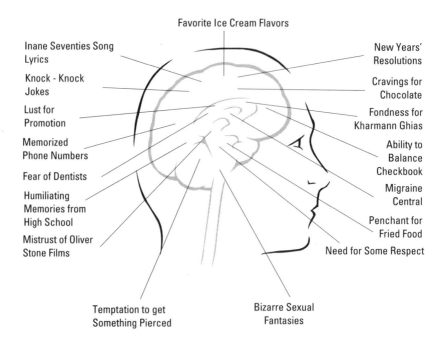

Favorite Ice Cream Flavors

Inane Seventies Song Lyrics

New Years' Resolutions

Knock - Knock Jokes

Cravings for Chocolate

Lust for Promotion

Fondness for Kharmann Ghias

Memorized Phone Numbers

Ability to Balance Checkbook

Fear of Dentists

Migraine Central

Humiliating Memories from High School

Penchant for Fried Food

Mistrust of Oliver Stone Films

Need for Some Respect

Temptation to get Something Pierced

Bizarre Sexual Fantasies

Human

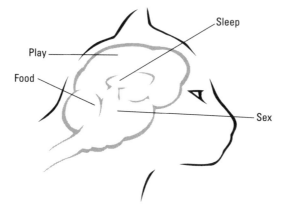

Cat

HOW HUMANS SEE YOU

HOW YOU REALLY ARE

Cat Mythology

> Only imbeciles do not know that
> all cats have a pact with the Devil.
> —*L'Evangile du Diable*

CATS ARE INSTRUMENTS OF THE DEVIL

Europeans in the Middle Ages associated cats with paganism, as witches' familiars or magical servants, witches in another form, marking a path to the Devil or even an embodiment of Satan himself. Witches were even killed with their cats.

As if this weren't enough, cats were thought to cause storms and wreck ships, desecrate crucifixes and turn beer sour. Many thought ridding the world of cats would rid them of ills, and cat stew became popular. But all they managed to rid themselves of was their most effective rat predator, and exacerbated the plagues by the subsequent proliferation of rodent-carried fleas.

In 1344, the entire population of Metz, Germany, was overtaken by an epidemic of St. Vitus' Dance. A pious knight-at-arms, presumably wanting to have a good laugh at all these people flailing around, visited and took a room at an inn. There he found a black cat sitting in the fireplace, staring at him. The knight promptly made the sign of the cross and lunged for his sword. The cat is supposed to have spat blasphemies and disappeared into thin air. (As if any sane animal would stay and be decapitated.) Predictably, Mr. Knight thought he'd seen the Devil, and when the town was miraculously cured the next day he told the town magistrates and they organized a ritual cat burning.

Every eve of St. John thereafter, thirteen living cats were thrown on a huge bonfire. These barbaric barbecues, the Fires of St. John, lasted 429 years, when in 1773 a Mme d'Armentières obtained us a reprieve. To this day, many a cat still gives up a little prayer to the great Madame, as it appreciates the distance between itself and the living room fire.

BLACK CATS ARE LUCKY

Because of the silly satanic associations, most countries believe a black cat crossing one's path is unlucky. The British, cleverly ignoring this slander, think it leads to *good* luck. This superstition appears to date from the writings of one Samuel Twerfle, an English manure-spreader's apprentice whom church records show died in Buggersby, Shropshire, in 1408. Twerfle was apparently obsessed with a neighbor's black cat, who tended to appear at his window. Whenever it did, Mrs. Twerfle suddenly seemed unusually interested in "performinge her nuptyal expectationnes," which endeared the cat to Samuel.

Later, Sam changed his mind when the same cat tangled itself in his ankles, causing him to become deeply immersed in his work. But by then the damage was done, his rumors had spread abroad, and the black cat's good luck was legend, at least in Britain. Other countries are still hampered by the old medieval superstitions of evil.

CATS SUCK THE BREATH OUT OF BABIES

It's true that we cats like to curl up on warm spots, and if the origin of that warmth is a human face we don't mind. It's quite possible that once or twice a cat may have accidentally suffocated a child, but it's more likely that crib death was just blamed on the family pet. Besides, it's only *adult* faces that are big enough to comfortably sit on.

CATS INVENTED HATHA YOGA

An old Indian story describes how a young prince named Hatha was having trouble concentrating on his difficult Karma Yoga meditation exercises.

(Karma Yoga involves getting in touch with one's previous incarnations and teaching *them* how to meditate too.) To clear his mind he went for a walk in the woods and came across a cat, sitting straight on a tree stump.

When he asked the cat how she could meditate so peacefully, she showed him how she stretched each muscle, twisting and arching, tensing and relaxing until her whole body was at rest and released from distractions.

Every day the prince returned and learned the cat's technique, eventually spreading his knowledge to others as Hatha's Yoga. In fact, he opened a chain of Hatha Yoga centers throughout Asia, becoming rich, famous and fat. Meanwhile the poor cat, though superbly relaxed, died from malnutrition in the forest.

CATS HAVE A SIXTH SENSE
Only six? Cats have *dozens* of senses, not to mention more *common* sense than most animals. Our sense of smell tells us what we're near without seeing it, exactly how far away it is, whether it's edible, and even when it last had a bath. Our vision enables us to see in bright sunlight, dim light, next to no light, and even red-light districts. Our sense of balance is so refined that we rarely put a foot wrong (and we can't even *see* two of them), even in the most delicate of situations. Well, hot tin roofs aside.

Okay—we're not exactly big on a sense of *humor*, but you can't have everything.

A CAT HAS NINE LIVES
This misconception probably stems from our ability to land on our feet, often narrowly escaping becoming purr purée. (But only if we have time

to turn around in midair so our feet are down. Paradoxically, a longer fall, within reason, is safer than a very short one.) This gave rise to the belief that cats have the power to cheat death. But stay away from those who wish to test this.

CATS CAN SEE IN THE DARK
Cat's eyes are designed to operate with far less light than human eyes, which makes us seem to the superstitious to be able to see in total darkness, our eyes appearing to glow from the reflection of what little light

there might be. (Primates, being by their nature daytime creatures, are incapacitated by the dark and remain afraid of the night.) Nor are cats usually hampered by the unfortunate mechanism that makes rabbits and deer freeze like statues in the face of dangers like car headlights, turning them into road pizza.

This plus the fact that we have no collarbones in order to facilitate the navigation of narrow, dark areas, and that our whiskers are the width of the body so we can find our way around even when blind made cats appear endowed with supernatural powers.

We *are* supernatural, of course. Supernaturally beautiful.

CURIOSITY KILLED THE CAT
We cats are relentlessly, incorrigibly, wonderfully curious. Originally a positive survival trait used for tracking prey and exploring, our peculiarly intense feline inquisitiveness can now have, in some situations, the opposite value. Every day meddling kitties meet untimely ends by being in the wrong place at the wrong time: under cars, under car hoods, in trash cans prior to pickup, fooling with the prop of the grand piano lid, etc. In our focus on the fascination of the moment we can sometimes lose sight of the larger picture. Like the train coming.

CATS LOVE MILK
Actually, only a few of us can tolerate lactose. Milk gives the rest of us diarrhea in a major way. If you value your carpet it's wise, therefore, to not

be too liberal with the cowjuice until you know to which group your cat belongs.

CATS CAN FIND THEIR WAY HOME OVER GREAT DISTANCES
Countless examples of this ability are recorded, and not all can be dismissed as the mere following of a scent trail.

An army sergeant was transferred from Kokomo, Indiana, to Augusta, Georgia, and took his cat by train with him. The cat made it back

to its original home, a distance of 700 miles, in three weeks. If you've ever been to Augusta, you'll understand what motivated this clever creature.

Moumousse was lost during his "owner's" holiday in Maine-et-Loire, France. Ten months later he returned to his master's house in Doubs, 465 miles away. And why not? Moumousse had fifteen lovers there.

And **Sugar**, a cream semi-Persian living in Anderson, California, was left behind with a neighbor when her family moved to Oklahoma. Fourteen months later, Sugar had somehow crossed half a continent—1,500 miles—to be reunited with them. Quite a trek, Sugar. Hope it was worth it.

Then there was **Chat Beau**, who traveled 300 miles from Lafayette, Louisiana, to Texarkana, Texas, in four months. **Pooh**, two years old, 200 miles between Newman, Georgia, and Wellford, South Carolina. **Smoky**, 417 miles from Tulsa, Oklahoma, to Memphis, Tennessee, in twelve months. **Rusty**, who managed the 950 miles from Boston, Massachusetts, to Chicago, Illinois. **Howie**, 1,000 miles across the Australian Outback to Adelaide. And **McCavity**, who trekked 500 miles from Cumbernauld, Scotland, to Truro, Cornwall.

Currently being investigated is the iron in the cat's body working as a kind of compass. Not under investigation, unfortunately, is the iron *will* of felines to be in comfort. How long does it take for humans to grasp that if we don't like it, we're outta there?

CATS CAN READ MINDS

This superstition possibly stems from the observation that cats are the only domestic animal that can look a human in the eye without flinching. But far from being a result of telepathy, it is a result of supreme *apathy*. Nothing could conceivably interest us *less* than the contents of an ape's mind, which we consider somewhat intellectually inferior.

Ancient Britons believed that if you gazed into a cat's eyes you could see into the spirit world—an inheritance, perhaps, from the Egyptians, who were fascinated with cat's eyes and whose word for the animal, *mau*, meant "to see." Personally, though, we'd rather not be stared at, spirit world or no. It's upsetting to be confronted at such close quarters by such vacancy.

IT'S BAD LUCK TO CROSS A STREAM WITH A CAT IN YOUR ARMS

This inane French proverb isn't too hard to understand. You might as well say it's bad luck to light a match in a firework factory. Anyone with a modicum of smarts knows that nearly all cats hate water. (There are exceptions, but we don't talk about that side of the family.) Therefore, if you're foolish enough to try to carry a cat across a large body of the stuff you'd better be prepared for some serious lacerations. The cat would obviously be concerned that the human, whom we consider more than a little uncoordinated, would drop it. And we prefer our water measured in bowlsful, thanks.

THE LYNX CAN SEE THROUGH WALLS

During the Middle Ages, several strange legends spread through Europe about the lynx. Apart from its supposed x-ray vision it was also thought to be huge and its urine to crystallize into gemstones, which shows how few people can have actually seen one. We can presume some medieval lynx pee-pursuers to have been severely disappointed. You might want to check that amber necklace, though.

THE MANX ORIGINALLY HAD A TAIL

According to legend, the Manx was late to the launch of Noah's Ark, and Noah accidentally slammed the door on its gloriously bushy tail.

Assuming for the moment that the story of Noah's Ark is true, it's extremely unlikely that any self-respecting cat would be late to get aboard. For a start, since we hate water it's not hard to guess that one of us would

do anything to avoid being caught in a worldwide *flood* of the revolting stuff. Secondly, while Noah is said to have included only *pairs* of animals, any cat would be smart enough to calculate that it wouldn't be long before there were plenty more than just two each of the rats and mice aboard, and wouldn't have missed the chance of such captive chow.

CATS CAN PREDICT EARTHQUAKES

Cats often do anticipate earthquakes because our refined senses and sensitive whiskers can detect vibrations long before the Bigs get an inkling that

something's wrong. By the time they're being bombarded by flying saucepans we're usually safely out the window or under the bed. (**Toto**, living in the foothills of Vesuvius, gave his hosts so much warning of the volcano's impending eruption that all escaped safely.)

Prior to recent . . . uh . . . *cat*aclysms in California, groups of shrewd cats apparently got together and jumped freights out of state, hitchhiked on excursion buses to Vegas, and stowed away on cruise ships to Acapulco.

CAN OPENER CLASS

THE NINE LIVES OF A CAT

Ding dong, bell
Pussy's in the well
—Traditional English children's rhyme

1 **The Playful Life**
Lost to playing with objects, like lawnmowers, that didn't play back.

2 **The Curious Life**
Lost to inquisitiveness about situations, like the open oven door, that should never have been looked into.

3 **The Territorial Life**
Lost in battle with other, bigger, meaner, cats.

4 **The Exploring Life**
Lost to motor vehicles while seeing if the grass really is greener.

5 **The Macho Life**
Lost in battle with a psychotic dog that wasn't afraid of claws.

6 **The Sporting Life**
Lost by falling into a river while reaching for those fascinating little fish.

7 **The Skydiving Life**
Lost in misjudging the distance between the fifteenth-floor apartment and street level.

8 **The Medical Life**
Lost in battle with those annoying stowaways, the internal parasites.

9 **The Senior Citizen Life**
Lost to old age, passing on to that Big Lap in the Sky.

THE FIRST AND ONLY EXPERIMENT WITH CAT SLEDS

CAT YEARS

Nothing's more playful than a young cat,
nor more grave than an old one.
—Thomas Fuller

This chart shows the approximate correlations between cat and human years.
(Sorry—the traditional multiplication of the cat's age by seven doesn't work.)

Felis catus		Homo sapiens
1	infancy-adolescence	15
2	youth	25
4	early middle age	40
7	late middle age	50
10	senior	60
15	getting on a bit	75
20	definitely pushing it	105
30	forget it	120

Average lifespan: ten years. Average time awake: three years.

Longest substantiated lifespan: thirty-six years.

IDENTIFYING YOUR CAT'S MOOD

Gaze with those bright languid segments
green, and prick those velvet ears—but prythee do not
stick thy latent talons in me . . .
—John Keats, *To Mrs. Reynolds' Cat*

Contented

Washtime

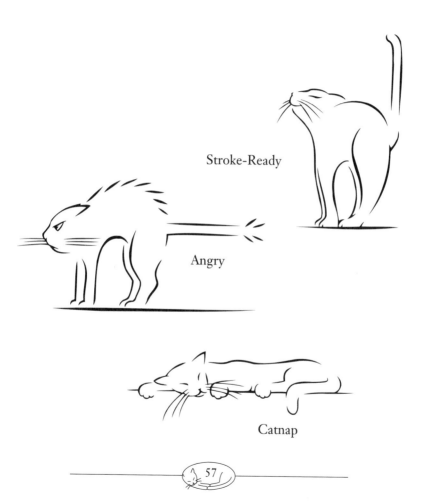

Stroke-Ready

Angry

Catnap

Ready to Pounce

Frisky

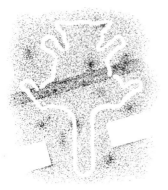

Careless

EAROGRAPHY

Happy, or at Least
Not *Un*happy

Angry

Frightened, or Scottish Fold

Listening to
Something Behind

TAILOGRAPHY

Self-expression with your caudal appendage

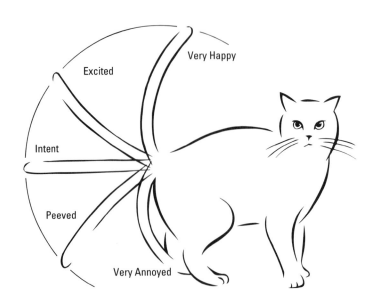

The Basic Positions

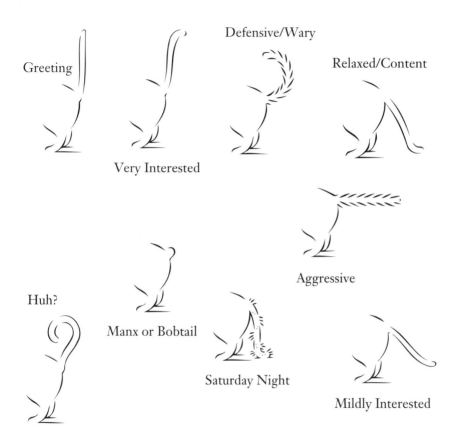

Greeting

Very Interested

Defensive/Wary

Relaxed/Content

Aggressive

Huh?

Manx or Bobtail

Saturday Night

Mildly Interested

WHISKEROGRAPHY

Vibes from the ol' vibrissae

English

Louis XIV

Military

Punk, Rex or Too Near the Stove

Male Mating Display

CAT DIET

Do cats eat bats? . . . Do bats eat cats?
—Lewis Carroll

Evil-smelling things in
    overpriced little cans
Mice and rats
Squirrels, small rabbits,
    gophers
Birds (especially pets)
Fish (especially pets)
Spiders, beetles, flies,
    butterflies, moths

Frogs
Bubbles
Wool
Garbage
Paper
Expensive shoes, belts
Shoelaces
Flowers, houseplants
Herbs in the windowbox

Anything that moves in an interesting way.

TWENTY STEPS TO A FITTER FELINE

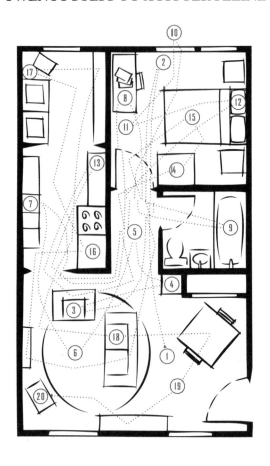

CAT AEROBICS

Kittens—are you living a full feline life?
Work off that widening waist with this twenty-step program.

1. Make sure humans are out

2. Spray bedroom

3. Stretch by scratching newest piece of furniture

4. Knock over vase, sniff flowers

5. Drag flowers around rooms, eat one

6. Vomit on expensive rug

7. Drink from tap, unroll all toilet tissue

8. Scatter papers on desk

9. Nap

10. Sneak out and catch bird or mouse

11. Maim and play with animal

12. Sneak back, leave dead animal in prominent position

13. Nap

14 Climb into wardrobe and shed hair on dress clothing

15 Relieve self on comforter

16 Nap

17 Hide and ignore humans upon return, until fed

18 Climb onto lap(s), submit to stroking

19 Swat indifferently at little jingly mouse toy

20 Curl up on TV, obscuring screen with tail

5

Catalog of Famous Felines

I call my kittens Shall and Will
because no one can tell them apart.
—Christopher Morley

CAT ACTORS

The most famous feline thespian in the United States is **Morris**, the "finicky" cat from the 9 Lives cat food commercials, who died in 1978 and was in turn replaced with Morris II. His British counterpart is **Arthur**, star of thirty Spillers Kattomeat commercials, in which he magnificently scooped cat food out of a can from 1966 to 1975. He died in 1976 and was succeeded by Arthur II.

CARTOON CATS

Because of our wonderful personalities, we cats are often immortalized in popular art, most notably cartoons. **Krazy Kat**, by George Herriman, graced Hearst Newspapers beginning in 1910. **Felix**, attributed to Pat Sullivan in the 1920s, was the first sound cartoon and became more popular than Charlie Chaplin, Harold Lloyd or Buster Keaton. **Sylvester**, whose first film screened in 1944, was actually awarded an Oscar in 1947. (It was Tweetie-Pie, the canary in his films, who is renowned for saying, "I tawt I taw a puddy tat!") There's also **Tom** of the hundreds of Tom and Jerry films. **Fritz the Cat**, a tougher, more streetwise feline, was first drawn by Robert Crumb in *Comix* and filmed by Ralph Bakshi in both 1972 and 1974. Currently, there's the famous (or perhaps infamous) **Garfield**, by Jim Davis, who created his insightful character in the United States in 1978.

CHARMION

We know next to nothing about Cleopatra's cat, but there's irony in Cleo having been a cat lover. A Roman soldier accidentally killed a cat in Egypt (where cats were, of course, revered), was tortured, dragged through the town and hanged. This triggered a war between the two countries, ending in the deaths of Cleopatra and her Roman lover Mark Antony.

THE CHESHIRE CAT

In Lewis Carroll's *Alice in Wonderland*, the Cheshire Cat gives Alice skewed advice through riddles. It appears grin-first and leaves grin-last, and though fictional, serves as a symbol of the cat's intelligence and sly cunning. Also, perhaps, our tendency to patronize.

DICK WHITTINGTON'S CAT

In the early fifteenth century little Dickie came from Gloucestershire to seek his fortune in London. Some versions of the story say his cat went with him, others that all he could afford from his meager scullion's wages was a cat to keep his garret rat-free. Anyway, when one day the other servants put up money to invest in their employer's trading ship, Dick contributed his only possession—his cat.

Upon its arrival at one of the Spice Islands, the cat promptly cleaned up the king's ratbag of a palace, and the grateful ruler gave the cat's "owner" a fortune in return for the continued services of the cat.

Dick went on to thrice become Lord Mayor of London, but not much is ever said about the cat's later life on the island. Actually the clever creature was pregnant when she arrived, and went on to give birth to several striking litters, who spread her line throughout the East, the descendants of which are now imported back into the West at exorbitant prices.

GRAYMALKIN

One of the spirits invoked to serve the witches at the beginning of Shakespeare's *Macbeth*, this cat doesn't appear much, being more of a symbolic, magic prop. Its role perpetuates the myth of cats being somehow evil, but then what would you expect from Scotland, where peasants up to the end of the Middle Ages were authorized to kill us and use our fur for clothing.

Graymalkin is only referred to once again by: *Thrice the brinded* [brindled—tabby] *cat hath mew'd.*

A cat of another kind is mentioned later in: *Add thereto a tiger's chaudron* [entrails], *For the ingredients of our cauldron.*

(A contrived rhyme if ever we've heard one.) Grimalkin has been a moniker for an old she-cat or, by extension, a spiteful old woman since 1605.

MANEKI-NEKO

Famous in Japan, Maneki (*Neko* means *cat*) is the small female cat who lures and enchants, bringing happiness and good luck. She is nearly always shown with a paw raised in greeting and benediction, and is the model for the phenomenally successful "Hello Kitty" line of charms and toys. Ceramic Maneki-Nekos are given to new business- and homeowners to attract good fortune and prosperity to the establishment.

PUSS-IN-BOOTS

In this 1697 story by Charles Perrault, a witty and flamboyant cat manages through its exploits to defeat a giant, make a peasant boy into the Marquis of Carabas, and allows him to marry a princess. Perrault adapted tales dating from Italian, Arabic and Sanskrit sources, showing the persistence of the belief that cats bring luck and good fortune.

SCHRÖDINGER'S CAT

Erwin Schrödinger, Nobel prize-winning physicist, described a hypothetical paradox linking the fate of a cat to the state of a simple quantum system.

A cat, he proposed, is placed in a box containing a bottle of poison, and the poison is released with a 50/50 probability linked to the outcome of a quantum event such as the decay/non-decay of a radioactive atom, or the up/down spin of an electron.

The laws of physics state that *until an observer looks in the box* the quantum system is in a hybrid of all possible states. Is the cat, therefore, also in a hybrid dead/alive state until observed?

Personally, we think the man should've been reported to the SPCA. Hypothetical or not, this is an experiment of extreme cruelty, and should never have been suggested in case some literal-minded physics student actually tries it.

TABITHA

In June of 1994 Tabitha and her sister Pandora were traveling in their respective cat carriers (or in Pandora's case, presumably a box) on a flight from New York to Los Angeles.

On arrival, only Pandora was where she was supposed to be. Tabitha had escaped somewhere, and for twelve days became a kind of *claws célèbre* as dozens of humans searched for her.

She was eventually located, two pounds lighter, after traveling 32,000 miles via San Juan and Miami, by a psychic who had predicted her whereabouts in the cargo area ceiling.

THE ORIGINAL TOM

Prior to 1760 male cats were called "Ram" cats, and then along came Tom the Cat in *The Life and Adventures of a Cat*. Were it not for this timely publication, we'd still be stuck with being known as either Rams or Dams, blunt and offensive terms referring solely to our reproductive roles. Sometimes one can still hear the term, "That dam cat," but this is luckily a rare and archaic holdover from the past.

WHITE HEATHER

Queen Victoria's cat is thought to have triggered the monarch's famous "We are not amused," when caught toying with Prince Albert's toupee. *Then there are the famous humans who professed to never be without their faithful felines . . .*

Sesostris, an Ethiopian, is said to have been the person who brought cats into Egypt after the conquest of Nubia. The **Egyptians** then worshipped the cat goddess *Bastet* (or Pasht, from which it is said we get *puss*), daughter of Isis and Osiris, from 3000 B.C. Bastet reigned 2,000 years, during which it was illegal, upon pain of death, to smuggle cats out of the country. **Cleopatra** modeled her eye makeup on the eyes of a cat.

In the Middle Ages a short-lived cult grew up around the Norse goddess of love **Freyia**, Freyja or Freya, who had two black cats pulling her chariot. This unfortunately just fueled (literally) more persecution, at a time when any religion other than Christianity was pronounced Pagan and attacked.

Mohammed truly appreciated cats. It's said that once, rather than disturb his favorite *Muezza* as she slept in his arms, he cut off his sleeve. Muezza awoke and bowed in thanks, and Mohammed passed his hand three times down her back in blessing, giving all cats henceforth immunity from the dangers of falling.

Although popular with **Buddhists**, the cat is not included in Buddhist writings allegedly because one of our kind happened to fall asleep during Buddha's funeral. Well, we all loved the man, but what did they expect? Those festivities just went on for ever. There's a limit to how many gongs and orange robes one can take, after all.

Pliny the Elder wrote about cats, as did **Cicero**, the Roman orator of the first century B.C. **Leonardo da Vinci** understandably loved us too, and **Isaac Newton** paid us the honor of inventing the cat flap, or cat door (probably at the request of his cat master), and was knighted for his brilliance. Whereas **Julius Caesar, Alexander the Great, Henry III of France, Napoleon Bonaparte** and **Adolf Hitler** are said to have hated us, which goes to show we're only disliked by those who should themselves be despised.

Owen Gould, British consul general in Bangkok, was given two Siamese cats by the King of Siam in 1884, and when Gould shipped them back to England he triggered a fashion.

Wordsworth, Tennyson, Coleridge, Byron, Twain, Keats, Swinburne, Sir Winston Churchill, Admiral Nelson, Cardinals Wolsey and Richelieu, Borges, Wells, Arnold, Hardy, James, Sand, Hugo, Poe, Colette, Lear, Zola, T. S. Eliot, Sir Walter Scott and **the Brontë sisters** would only work with their cats around, no doubt to help critique their creations and help with the difficult bits. **Hemingway's** home in Key West, Florida, is still full of felines.

And many a U.S. president has shrewdly kept a cat at his side in the White House. **George Washington, Rutherford B. Hayes, Thomas**

Jefferson, Herbert Hoover and **Abraham Lincoln** all required a feline presence in the Oval Office. **Calvin Coolidge** had *Tiger* and *Blacky*, **Theodore Roosevelt** was advised by *Slippers* and *Tom Quartz*, **Gerald Ford** consulted *Shan*, and **Jimmy Carter** relied upon his daughter Amy's *Misty Malarky Ying Yang*. **John F. Kennedy** was sadly a touch allergic but nevertheless kept around Caroline's *Tom Kitten* (and possibly a supply of antihistamines), and **Bill Clinton** of course sports *Socks*, the First Cat.

THE CAT IN ART

Prehistoric
Lascaux Caves, France c.1300 B.C.

Egyptian
Limestone stela, Eighth Dynasty, c.2276 B.C.

Greek
Amphora by Mykattides c.510–500 B.C.

Roman
Capital from the Temple of Felixus c.300 B.C.

Maya
Petroglyph c.700

Indian
The God Sastht, Punjai, c.1000

Renaissance
Leonardo da Vinci, pen and ink, c.1510

Cubist
Pablo Picatso, *La Derrière du Chat*, 1908

Futurist
Wasily Katdinsky, *Cat in Motion*, 1918

Modernist
Jackson Pollock, *Cat No. 5*, 1949

Cat Camouflage

Can the Ethiopian change his skin,
or the Leopard change his spots?
—*Bible*, Jeremiah

Far from being the random result of mixed genetic inheritance, feline markings are actually cunning adaptations to the modern world. Evolving faster than almost any other organism, each cat comes in a variety superbly and opportunistically suited to its environment.

Tabby/Mackerel/Agouti (brown and black in irregular stripes or blotches) to be able to hide among trees and bushes and pounce on unsuspecting birds.

Shorthaired White to blend with snow, fog, flour.

Spotted Tabby (Ocelot or Leopardlike) Bad wallpaper, polka-dot clothing.

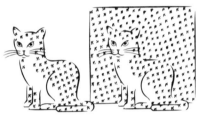

Chinchilla/White Persian (fluffy white), to sleep undisturbed among fur coats, pillows, angora sweaters, yetis, and on sheepskin seatcovers.

Black, or **Blue** (gray-blue) to be able to remain indistinguishable in cellars, trash cans, shadows and during nocturnal sexual laisons.

Solid Point
(Siamese/seal/chocolate/blue—pale gray or cream with black or brown face and paws) to merge with bamboo.

Tortoiseshell (red and black irregular patches) and **Calico** (tan and black patches), to be able to disguise ourselves in sock drawers, on half-dead lawns, badly-patched driveways, hospital operating-room floors and accidents in the kitchen.

CATANATOMY

The smallest feline is a masterpiece
—Leonardo da Vinci

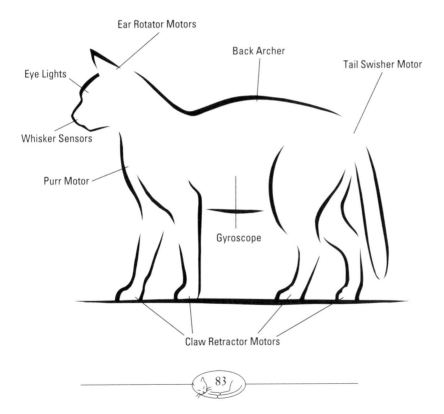

Ear Rotator Motors

Back Archer

Tail Swisher Motor

Eye Lights

Whisker Sensors

Purr Motor

Gyroscope

Claw Retractor Motors

CAT'S GUIDE FOR YOUNG CATS

> A kitten is so flexible that she is almost double; the hind
> parts are equivalent to another kitten with which the
> forepart plays. She does not discover that her tail belongs
> to her until you tread on it.
> —Henry David Thoreau

When bored, chew the edges of important documents.
When tense, chase tail.
When resentful, play noisily at three A.M.
When neglected, scratch something.
When perky, climb the curtains.
When horny, spray.
When hungry, stick nose in ear of sleeping host.
When lonely, meow incessantly.
When wanted, hide in remote, undiscoverable places.
When boisterous, tease a dog, or harass the hamster.
When offended, pee in houseplant pots, cupboards or shoes.
When curious, explore dumpsters.
When in trouble, purr.

English/Cattish Dictionary

If a man could be crossed with a cat,
it would improve man but deteriorate the cat.
—Mark Twain

*Though they tend to make a lot of them, few noises humans
make have much relevance, except for the following:*

Breakfast!
Time to eat.

Lunch!
Time to eat.

Dinner!
Time to eat.

**Mumble mumble Vet
mumble mumble**
Time to split.

Oooooh *darling!* Yes! *Yes!*
Time to investigate.

No!
OK, go ahead.

Mouse!
Time to hunt, then eat.

Kitty?
Time to ignore.

Here, KittyKittyKitty!
Time to hide.

Stop that!
That's nice, carry on.

Bad cat!
Good cat.

HOW WE SEE HUMANS

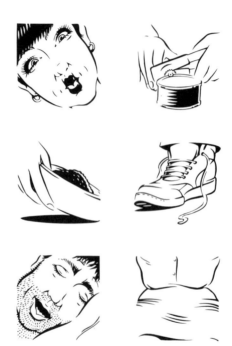

HUMANS VS. FELINES

Cats and monkeys, monkeys and cats—
all human life is there.
—Henry James

Humans	Cats
Need to wear clothes	Grow our own, thanks
Need to join spas	The whole house is our gym
Need to work for a living	Zzzzzzzzzzzzzzzz
Need long preambles to sex	Just get on with it
Need to sleep in beds	But *everything's* a bed, isn't it?
Need to use cosmetics	Always look good
Need to wash with water	Self-cleaning
Need to cook	Are fed
Need to think	Huh?

Predator!

Self-reliant like the cat—
that takes its prey to privacy,
the mouse's limp tail hanging like a shoelace from its mouth.
—Marianne Moore

Unlike the other slave animals, whose instincts, such as they are, have become decadent, corrupt or just atrophied into uselessness, cats remain what we always were: a pursuer, a raptor. Certainly we can manage without live food—some of us even prefer to—but in a split second we can still switch from Tabby to Tiger, Manx to Lynx. And this is not mere regression, either. We, the proud, direct descendants of *Felis silvestris libyca* never lost those instincts, and they lie latent behind our every liquid move, ready for resurrection.

As we pour ourselves through the garden fence we're padding across grasslands of which we are the landlord and everything else just tenants on sufferance. As we doze in front of the fire we're reliving our best catches. Our actions with the ball of wool are honing our attack reflexes, and only *seem* like playfulness. And every meal we eat reminds us of our primal directive. We will only ever be *semi*-civilized, and that's the way we like it.

So it should be no surprise to our host species that we revert occasionally, perhaps even regularly, to hunting mode. It's in our genes, our natures, our souls. Cats are natural selection's best land predator, kin to the air's eagle and the ocean's shark. Not for nothing is the lion known as the King of the Jungle (though it's the lion*ess* who does most of the killing). The cheetah, fastest of all land animals, was so effective that it was taken on hunts from the reigns of pharaoh to Medici. All across the world the animal kingdom has a healthy respect for the prowess of the Ocelot, Panther, Leopard, Puma, Jaguar.

Even in the quiet and safe domestic situation the oldest tom can still rouse himself for the inquisitive mouse. The nursing queen will leave her kindle of kittens to bring back samples of her skills.

And while we're all masters of the chase, some of our ranks have risen to exalted heights.

Minnie, of White City Stadium, London, dealt with 12,480 mice between 1927 and 1933. **Mickey**, guard of Shepherd & Sons, Ltd., Burscough, Lancashire, disposed of 22,000 mice in 23 years. And **Towser**, the much-missed mouser extraordinarie of Glenturret Distillery, Crieff, Perthshire, bagged 25,000 mice from 1963 to 1986.

And these are just the recorded, verified bags of recent years. Who knows how many rodents we disposed of for the Egyptians? Who can estimate how many more plague-carrying rats we could've spared Europe if not for that darkest of dark ages wiping out so many of our kind?

Foolishly, some societies have tried to control rodents without us. The Greeks tried weasels and stone martens before they realized these creatures killed everything, indiscriminately. And in thirteenth-century Japan they began to think that mere *representations* of cats would deter vermin, without the real thing. Bad move.

No, history has shown there really is no substitute for the domestic Cat, hunter on a small scale perhaps, but hunter supreme.

THE HUNT

For those weaned too early to have learned this from their mothers, here are the pertinent steps in becoming a working carnivore, Nature's predator par excellence:

1. Locate vermin.

2. Stalk to within striking distance.

3. Freeze and sneer.

4. Crouch down on front paws, raise butt.

5. Swish tail from side to side.

6. Narrow eyes.

7. Stutter and drool.

8. Pounce, biting neck of prey.

9. Waggle prey around.

10. If prey moves, slash with claws to prevent escape.
    If prey doesn't move, slash with claws to see if it still can.
    If prey still doesn't move, go to **14**.

11 Play with prey, releasing and recapturing at least six times.

12 [optional] Toss prey in air and catch.

13 Pretend to have lost interest.

14 Eat prey, or

15 Eat *some* of prey and leave remainder on pillow.

Reigning Cats and Dogs

The cat, an aristocrat, merits our esteem, while the dog
only . . . got his position by low flatteries.
—Alexandre Dumas

Dogs became pets around 45,000 years ago by hanging around campfires
and giving up their individuality in return for a few scraps of gristle and
the odd bone or two. On the other hand, though cats appeared on earth
over ten *million* years ago, we *never* gave up our identity.

Experts in animal behavior might try to tell you that the difference
lies in the genes: dogs evolved as pack animals who bring down their prey
in cooperative groups, and so were programmed to get along with others.
Cats, on the other hand, are by nature solitary hunters, and so are genetically unequipped for social behavior.

This, as any cat knows, is errant nonsense. Cats can behave socially

when we want to—we're just shrewder. Recognizing our dog cousins' enslavement for what it was, we adopted our "I'm doing you a favor by just allowing you to house and feed me" attitude. (In fact, it is now acknowledged that we *invented* attitude, along with yoga and mood swings.) Why else would it have taken us *forty thousand years* longer than dogs to hang out with humankind? No, the feline species chose humans to use as hosts, not masters, and at best are only ever houseguests and never slaves. We're just as social as any other species, but where dogs idolize, we patronize. Dogs fawn; we scorn. Besides, dogs made the classic army mistake—they *volunteered*.

So cats made a concerted effort to train humans as pets, and it just took us a long time. As already mentioned, direct methods—the outright rounding up of Stone Age man and hoping they would perform as domestics—just resulted in the extinction of the Neanderthal. Eventually cats decided on our present eminently successful method—*pretending* to be pets, while using hominids as unwitting serfs.

In this manner cats now only have to hunt for fun, as anyone who's ever seen a cat playing with a mouse will attest. No longer do we need to work for a living, since our food comes out of cans, and our longest trek is now from the top shelf of the entertainment center to the patch of sun on the kitchen windowsill.

Dogs, on the other hand, have to sit, stay, fetch, carry, lie down, beg, shake hands, roll over, play dead, herd, guard, point, sniff, retrieve and all those other mundane duties of their kind. They've become an *appendage* to man, subject to his whims and orders. Besides, they get their ears in their food.

But have we cats still sold out our independence in choosing human hosts? This is the subject of ongoing debates in feline circles, sometimes leading to those heated discussions in the middle of the night outside your bedroom window. Are dogs better off? Have canines done better out of their association? We have only one word in response:

Poodles.

CANINES VS. FELINES

Dogs	Cats
Howl.	Yowl.
Can be trained to do tricks.	Talk to my agent.
Friendly, cooperative.	Selfish, indifferent.
Can detect and deter intruders.	Will allow intruders to stroke, then yawn and nap.
Will mark everything, forever.	Will spray everything, until fixed.
Will eat until they puke, if allowed.	Will only eat what we need, usually.
Can herd animals.	Will attack animals.
Can be taken for walks.	Walk? Why? It's raining.
Want to please.	Want to be waited on.
Will fetch.	Moi? Surely you jest.
Yap, bark, yelp, growl, slaver, pant.	Please. How crass.
Beg.	Tickle my tummy, would you? Ahh, that's it. Just there.

THE FIRST AND ONLY EXPERIMENT WITH
GUIDE CATS FOR THE BLIND

Types of Cat "Owner"

. . . This is the cat
That killed the rat
That ate the malt
That lay in the house that Jack built.
—*Nurse Truelove's New Year's Gift*, 1755

FAMILIES

This is by far the most common situation in which a self-respecting cat can find him- or herself. There are always plenty of dramas and lots of stimulation to keep you active. Dealing with small children, as described above, can be traumatic, but this is on the whole a gratifying nest type since there's always attention to be had from someone. At least one of the family is generally a soft touch and can be manipulated relentlessly. In fact, for cats with large appetites it's often possible to elicit meals from more than one human, using stealth and cunning.

Families also tend to possess a *back yard* that you can claim as your own, stalking suburban songbirds and small pets that next-door neigh-

bors mistakenly let loose for walkies. Don't bother with the tortoises, though.

SENIORS
These are often disproportionately women, since the human female seems to kill off the male after a while and live alone. Perhaps she eats him, we're not sure. But anyway, we are supremely important to these aging bipeds, since they stay in the nest a lot and need our affectionate company to save them from turning into potatoes.

Hold down the tripping and zooming with these types—they're frail and may not recover from any sudden surprises. Though predictable, they can be touchingly loving and while they tire easily, they still enjoy serving. Besides, they always have balls of yarn to attack. And you can always sneak out occasionally for a bit of fun.

CAREER COUPLES

Lately more and more couples are choosing to stay childless and just work a lot. In the good old days there was either one at home most of the time, or at least not too much of the day spent away by both. But this new system means you'll have the nest to yourself an uncomfortable amount.

You can try the trashing techniques covered earlier, but this obsessive need to work is displacement behavior that stems from their not having a little servant or two to focus their energies, and as a consequence it goes deep and is difficult to undo.

If possible, supply them with a batch or two of yours, which may make them more homebound. But chances are your reproductive capabilities have been tampered with. If so, you may have to make your loneliness known by pitiful mewing, forlorn gazing from the window as they leave, and hanging out with any stuffed animal you can find. With any luck this will result in their bringing in another cat as a companion.

SINGLE MEN

Some men are quite adequate domestics, as nurturing as any female, family or senior. Others, however, are frustrated *dog* persons—you can tell: they're embarrassed at living with a cat because they don't consider it macho enough. Some part of them really wants a rottweiler or pit bull, and they probably either inherited you from an old girlfriend or a mom that took the dirt nap, or just thought you'd be less trouble. It's up to you to make this kind of human's life miserable, in the hope that you'll be transferred to a home with a more amenable servant.

Men, despite what they think of themselves, are really not too bright, and can be toyed with in most rewarding ways. Chew holes in his under-

pants (the clean ones, naturally), and since men place a lot of importance on their vehicles, shred the car upholstery next time he tries to take you somewhere.

But save your worst manners for those times he's trying to get intimate with his lover. When he puts his face on hers, leap on them hissing and spitting, scratching her clothing. This should shatter the romantic ambiance sufficiently, but if more is needed go berserk in the bedroom. Use your "baby being tortured" voice and fling yourself around the walls like a demented bat.

The human male will be mortified, the female will reject him as a prospective partner, and he should either (a) treat you better, or (b) give you to someone who will. Of course, there's always (c) get violent, in which case you'll have to find a new nest as quickly as felinely possible.

FARMERS

A rural domain can provide a most beneficial life for a feline, as long as you like catching your food on the hoof, as it were, as will probably be expected of you.

Your territory will be large, there'll be lots of big, dumb animals to spook and annoy, and rodents by the barnful. Of course, if you're one of those urbane, effete "I only eat out of cans" types this will be quite an adjustment, but a worthwhile one. (Food that wriggles is so much more fun.)

This is, after all, closer to our ancestral habitat than some one-bedroom cubicle in a building that should've been condemned five administrations ago. Then again, a few scruffy fields of alfalfa and corn ain't exactly the foothills of Kilimanjaro either, but at least it's a kind of freedom not found in the city.

Drawbacks are burrs in the fur, ticks in the ears and becoming a kind of bus for fleas, but what are humans for if not for grooming? Those opposable thumbs are useful for something, after all.

This is also a situation in which we come up against creatures with almost equally powerful predator skills, and who can catch us off-guard if we're not careful. Foxes, large psychotic and/or very hungry dogs, and in some countries coyotes, wolves, wolverines, hyenas and skunks should be steered well clear of. We may be smarter, but they don't care that we're more edified, only that we're edible.

TEENS

Living with teenage or twentysomething Bigs is usually a serious mistake, since at those ages they're throwbacks to the barbarian. They'll forget to feed you, change the litterbox, or put down fresh water. In fact, they'll often forget to come home for days, and when they finally do you'll wish they hadn't. They'll bring over all kinds of lowlife friends, have loud parties until all hours and play noises of indescribable abrasiveness.

If you find yourself in this kind of predicament your best bets are twofold. One, the obvious, is to move. The second is to manage to dye yourself an unnatural color and, if possible, trim or singe one side of your fur radically. By this method you'll brand yourself cool, or at least odd, and they'll include you in their circle of friends instead of thinking of you as just some domestic obligation.

GANGS, BIKERS, ETC.
Sadly, these kinds of humans embody the worst traits of teens, small boys and single men combined. If this suits your temperament, fine, but many of us dislike drinking rainwater out of rusty hubcaps, defecating in an old tire and dumpster-dining on things like moldy ranch flavor chips and fish skins.

Better to try and find an old lady on one of her trips to and from the stores and latch on, in the hope that she'll take you home.

STRAY/HOMELESS
Not many of us choose the homeless life, but end up vagrant by default. And like other indigent creatures, once outside the pale of civilization it's difficult to reenter. Cats are a little better off than most in that we can still keep ourselves clean, and therein lies our salvation.

For those who pine after the soft suburban lifestyle, find an area you'd like to live in, isolate a houseful of humans you think could serve your purposes, preen carefully and adopt them with your winning, kittenish ways.

Play hard to get at first, so as not to seem too eager, then condescend to accept the occasional saucer of water. Then just hang around more and more until the children make a fuss if you leave. By that time you've won, and you can move in.

LABORATORY SCIENTISTS

Never, *ever*, go along with any humans wearing white coats or who smell of anesthetic, no matter how tasty their treats. Each year, cats by the million disappear into so-called "scientific establishments" and are never seen again. Rumors abound as to what actually happens inside, but whatever it is you don't want it to happen to you.

If you've had the misfortune to be born in one of these places, or taken when you were a kitten and too small to know what was going on, escape at all costs. If you can't get out of the cage, enlist the help of one of the chimps. They're related to humans and can figure out the locks.

CAT SOCIAL CLASSES

*Since a cat's social standing can't be identified by the way
it dresses and speaks, we can't solely be assessed by color
or length of coat. And since cats mate less discriminately
than humans, (after all, rich cats as well as poor all go out
to get in the family way, by any suitor that suits) the only
reliable identifying mark of social standing is thus our
name, which shows what kind of nest we're from.*

boudoir/show

The Pedigreed Ones: Polysyllabic names like Satinpennypus Amberglowmistmuff, Apricotcreaméclair Honeybuncurd, Fudgebucket Catnip Squitsmeister, Pastelpockets Downyheather, Jamdoughnut Heathburton, Scheherazade von Sandringham, Blancmangelette Bertinaboots, etc.

bohemian

Artsy or political names like Tolstoi, Isolde, Buxtehude, Warhol, Goethe, Thelonious, Che, Kierkegaard, Madame Bovary, Rasputin, Mao, Fibonacci, Schwartzenegger, etc.

house/family

Standard, honest cat names like Samantha, Smoky, Brandy, Fluffy, Whisky, Tiger, Cleo, Marmalade, Socks, Morris, Patches, Lady Di, etc.

farm

Dry, boring names like The Cat, Kitty, Fred, Jane, Turd, etc.

stray/alley

The most basic of labels: Hey you! Getouttahere! Shutthehellup! Whatthehellsthatracket! Etc.

Training Your Hosts, Part 2

For I will consider my cat Jeoffry.
For he is the servant of the Living God,
duly and daily serving Him.
. . . for he is of the tribe of Tiger.
—Christopher Smart, *Jubilate Agno*

THE CLAIMING OF CHAIRS

One of the many peculiarities of twolegs is the belief that chairs, sofas and stools are provided for *their* benefit. This typifies the pathetically limited understanding of their kind for the Great Hierarchy of Life, of which we are of course the zenith. While it's true that having only two legs and a re-markably clunky and inflexible skeleton means they must rest in specially-shaped receptacles (instead of, like *felidae*, anywhere we damn well please), always remember that *nothing* in the home is theirs.

If you ever suspect some benighted human seems to be thinking pro-prietorially about a particular chair, claim it for a few days at a stretch.

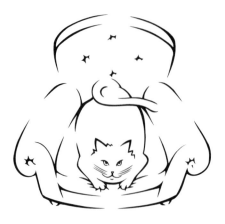

Scratch and hiss demoniacally if it attempts to sit on the chair while you're in residence, and you'll find in a few days they'll have forgotten they ever considered it their own. Or at least be too frightened to try it again.

TOYNESS

A key fact sadly lost by some of us on leaving the innocent bliss of kitten-hood is that *everything is a toy*. The most inanimate objects can be played with if you've retained the knack, from polystyrene packing peanuts to those flimsy undergarments in the bedroom (do humans actually *wear* this stuff?). Matchbooks, pencils, plants, cosmetics, condoms, credit cards, Ping-Pong balls, dentures—the list is endless. That alarm clock—isn't it a

giant silhouette of . . . a *mouse?* That glass thing—it's not a knickknack, it's a *cockroach!* Those shoelaces—*worms! Snakes!* Pounce! Kill! Eat!

Eyes glowing like amber coals behind slitted lids, the wiry muscles of Shere Khan the tiger flex beneath his flank as he leaps from the elephant grass and sinks his hunt-honed fangs into the—well, you get the picture.

And as for other creatures, they can be even more satisfying to fool around with. Who can forget the spectacular reaction of a caged bird when we stick our nose between the bars and display our teeth?* How delicious to bait a dog and then suddenly slash mercilessly at its fat, glossy nose. And members of *Homo sapiens*, of course, are endless fun to harass and confuse. They even recognize our play needs to such an extent that they order a bundle of fresh toy, called a *newspaper*, to be delivered for us every morning.

---

*Stay away from the parrot.

Never give up the playfulness that makes we cats such a joy to be around. Be creative. Suspend that boring belief in reality long enough to imbue anything with life and swat at it, drag it around, pounce on it and rip it to shreds.

Then, naturally, play with the shreds.

DISPLAYS OF AFFECTION

One of the many misunderstandings of our behavior is the human interpretation of what appears to them to be feline *affection*. We are truly loving (as duly noted under *Being the Source of Love*), but sometimes other actions can be mistakenly assumed to be affectionate. What looks to them like a fond snuggle by their four-legged friend is, of course, your *allomarking*—using the mouth, then forehead, cheek and entire length of your body to transfer scent from glands in your head and tail to your servant, now marked as your property. Scratching and clawing leaves scent from your paws too, proving in no uncertain terms to your myriad chums what's whose.

Another misunderstood action is licking. Instead of being what they read as an expression of love or devotion, we're just using our raspy tongue in racially remembered instincts. The obvious is the cleaning reflex—we are such fastidious creatures, after all. And humans *do* smell just a little, well, *overripe* at times. They've obviously lost the ability to lick themselves clean, though you can sometimes catch them licking each other. Some vestigial grooming behavior, presumably.

But another instinctive use of our tongue is stripping flesh from bone.

Now chances are you won't want to tear your domestics to bits, since good help is so hard to find these days, but licking nevertheless serves as a delicious reminder of our latent savagery.

THE NECESSITY OF SCRATCHING

A related issue is scratching, the overwhelming need to tatter something with our claws. Veterinarians try to tell our staff that scratching is not to *sharpen* claws but to dull and trim them, to remove old claw sheaths and reveal the new.

But as we know, scratching is another kind of territorial mark, as equally satisfying to deliver as the spray. Who of us hasn't experienced the thrill of developing one's own style of ripping ritzy fabric from the arm of the loveseat? What cat can deny itself the gouging of expensive wallpaper, costly cushions? What feline can decline the deep and damaging tear of nylons, lace curtains, silk dresses and shirts, the satisfying shred of a sock?

Your hosts will probably try to distract you with a scratching post/climbing tree—some tacky monstrosity of brightly colored acrylic shag stapled to a pole that they bought on sale at the pet shop and stuck behind the washing machine. It's traditional to ignore this and stay with what you started.

Try not to get carried away on some demented scratch-a-thon though, or the cruel bipeds will have your claws hacked out, and then you won't be able to climb or protect yourself on the street. It makes you wonder—if they don't want us to scratch they remove our claws; if they don't want us

to mate they take away our equipment. What if we eat too much? Will they have our tongues cut out? The Manx must've *really* pissed them off.

Just be thankful that those cat's eyes in the road are really just glass, and that catgut comes from sheep.

THE NEED FOR ZOOMIES
Bipeds often assume, because of our supreme ability to relax and relish the sensuousness of our surroundings, that we are slothful and indolent. Consequently it often becomes necessary to mount a display of your athletic powers just to put them in their place.

All this requires is to suddenly dash madly from room to room, book-case to ottoman, sink to sofa. Climb the Christmas tree, whack the blinds, chase toilet articles around the bathtub. In the middle of the night. And don't overlook the curtains in that Olympic spring from the ceiling. Not all the time, of course—no need to burn off too much energy unnecessarily—but more as a kind of punctuation to your usual languid existence.

Everybody knows a cheetah can reach speeds of 65 MPH during a chase, but did you know *Felis catus*, on hearing the can opener, has been clocked at 70 MPH in that mad dash between bedroom and kitchen?

But don't try this in the street. Humans, lethargic lumps that they are, drive everywhere in metal boxes they can barely control, have reflexes slower than those of a hippo, and *they* can't see in the dark.

USE OF LITTER BOX

It's quaint, but your hosts will expect you to defecate in a tray full of per-fumed aqua gravel parked conspicuously in the traffic flow of the house. This can be, needless to say, humiliating. To the descendants of Raj, whose muscular, tawny presence claimed the entire prairie as her pissoir, this is the ultimate in insult.

Humans also like to ignore the state of the litterbox until *their* senses are reminded it needs cleaning. But as every animal knows, their noses have de-generated to the point of uselessness, so what smells a little to them has been reeking to us for weeks. The usual punishment meted out for this negligence is random defecation on your part, in intimate areas like the bedroom.

ZOOMING

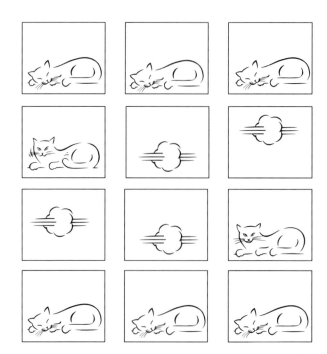

Luckily, most of them have heard rumors that from a genetically inherited survival traits we like to bury our wastes. This gives us the perfect pretext for spraying the offensive stuff all over the kitchen, bathroom, or wherever they've relegated our bodily functions.

THE MARKING OF TERRITORY
Those giant bipeds who run your house have little concept of territory. They can claim only the few cramped rooms you all inhabit, and even then the real owner is some bank. (Sometimes their children will make a pathetic effort to tag their blocks with spray cans, but this is typically crude. And occasionally a male can be seen identifying an alley after a few drinks, but this is random.) So it's not surprising that marking territory is outside their limited ken. Strangely, they tend to always urinate in the

same place, which doesn't serve to tell their friends anything about who they are or what they've been up to, as does our informative little message.

As a result they entirely miss our need to constantly renew our scents on the boundaries of our turf. (Otherwise the neighborhood would go, after all, to the dogs.) These olfactorily-challenged creatures can't comprehend that we may own the next *four* houses, half the street, a critical alley crossroad, and that these properties need *re*claiming regularly. Nor do they grasp that a tom's territory is *ten times* larger than a female's, and takes consequently ten times more effort to police it. (Not to mention ten times more urine.)

No, let's face it, they'll never be successfully trained in this, and you'll have to resign yourself to their noncomprehension every time you go out, come in, go out, come in and want to go out again. Exasperating, but there it is.

THE ART OF HIDING
Having great height has its advantages, which is why we keep humans around for reaching things on the top shelves, but one of the problems with being a giant is that you can't indulge in *hiding*, one of our most rewarding skills. Their children, of course, revel in it for as long as they can, but soon they grow too massive to ever be lost by anyone. Unfortunately.

We, on the other hand, are masters of magic, able to disappear at will. This is a useful knack when your servants require you for something that

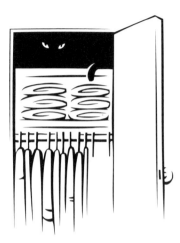

doesn't interest you, or in order to scold them for bad food, bad music, bad manners or some other indiscretion. And because of our compactness and flexibility our choices are endless: beds, boxes, laundry baskets and bags, shelves and drawers, closets, cars and cartons, pots and pans, roofs and gutters, chimneys and trees.

As a general rule, watch out for things with engines in them, things with dogs in them, things that are thrown out of windows, down chutes, mashed in big trucks or recycled. Also, try not to get too high in the trees, or you'll have to be rescued by men in funny hats from a big red ladder vehicle, and it's embarrassing.

SUFFERERS OF ALLERGIES

Some poor humans are handicapped with an inability to appreciate the feline race without sneezes, wheezes, watering eyes and a difficulty in breathing. This probably stems from some mutation or other genetic defect. You'll easily be able to recognize them: One day your servant will bring home a new lover and they'll cringe at the sight of you. All evening they'll try to keep as far away from you as they possibly can.

Don't worry. Offensive as is the mere presence of someone who can't treasure *us*, lords of the hearth that we are, these unfortunates can be easily dealt with. Once they're seated, jump in their lap, rub against them, scratch yourself with abandon and divest yourself of as much hair as you can muster. This will instantly ensure you'll never have to traffic with them again.

Occasionally you'll even come across a twolegs with an actual, full-blown *phobia* about us. These ailurophobes undoubtedly won't stick around for long, but while they're there, why not amuse yourself? Hide until they relax, then throw all your energy reserves into a prodigious leap at their face, jaws wide, preferably screeching.

THE FUN AND PITFALLS OF CURIOSITY

Our nests, since they're built and decorated by humans, always have lots of unnecessary bric-a-brac around. Their entire lives are full of clutter, and they don't seem to need, use, or even know why they bought many of the items.

Nevertheless, it's all fun to examine, as long as certain dangers are borne in mind. By all means be curious; just be circumspect about your inquiries. Calamities often await on balconies and stoves, in plastic bags and washing machines, near light bulbs, candles, fireworks and the iron. Rubber bands, pills, antifreeze, cigarettes, toads and pieces of tinsel are *not* edible. Chimneys are usually best to leave alone, as are office shredding machines, rocking chairs, fans, plastic bags, wasps and bees, cacti and electric pruning shears. Don't get your flea collar caught on something that might drive away, don't chew those attractive electric wires, and remember that some plants have been ignorantly kept around even though they're poisonous, so don't nosh on those either.

And finally, we've found from experience that the police kennels are definitely not worth investigating.

THE USE AND ABUSE OF TAIL (DOES NOT APPLY TO MANX AND BOBTAIL)

Your tail is not only your anchor, your counterbalance, but a limb capable of its own expressive gestural language. A kind of postural punctuation. Needless to point out, *Homo sapiens* doesn't sport this articulate appendage, and misunderstands its signals on animals that do.

It may take some time to educate your servants in its semaphore, and we have included some diagrams of general, emotional, tailography in the *Identifying Your Cat's Mood* section for this purpose.

But the tail is capable of more subtle meanings too. For instance, if you suspect you're being ignored at breakfast you can easily whip your tail from human nostril to granola and back again with no problem at all. As a statement of contempt, drag your tail across the face of an allergic biped or someone who smells of dog. As a casual remark of disdain, whack over an *objet d'art*—hopefully irreplaceable—or a vaseful of flowers. And as an expression of boredom, flick those car keys down the back of the cupboard where they won't be found for hours.

As always, watch out for locations or objects capable of amputation. And to the dangers listed under *Hiding* and *Curiosity*, add electric fires, the waste disposal, the kitchen cutting board at salad time, and the toaster.

THEORIES OF CONSPIRACY

Some non-cat admirers, probably those hostile *dog people*, think that cats are taking over.

It's true that our numbers have swollen to fifty-six million in the United States, with that of dogs only at fifty-one million. There are upwards of seven million cats in the United Kingdom (where we're in a *quarter* of the homes), and not nearly as many dogs. In France, felines are 7,500,000 strong, canines a measly 6,000,000. This means that in modern industrial cities there are at least 1,000 kitties per square mile.

But it's wrong to think of this as a conspiracy of specie-wide proportions. This is not an attempt at takeover of the so-called human world by felines—this is a *fait accompli*. We succeeded some time ago, and are now reaping the rewards of our subtle, bloodless coup, our intimate invasion.

We are installed permanently in their apartments, their condos, their villas. We are ensconced forever in their garages, on their roofs, at their fireplaces. Darwin was right, and humans have been surpassed by the true evolutionary leader, the Cat, and live under our benign felinocracy.

And the best part is that they don't even know it.

BEING THE SOURCE OF LOVE

Humans have a deep-seated need not only to *be* loved but to love back, and by far the greatest contribution catkind makes is the love we give them, and allow them to give us. They exchange it with each other too, but theirs is fragile and dependent on too many factors. Ours is unconditional.

Stroking us calms us both, so we're therapeutic. So much so, in fact, that we're employed in hospitals and nursing homes in Europe. The survival rate after a heart attack is higher in humans with a cat. Research even shows humans with a pet live longer. And why not? We give their lives meaning, focus. And we recharge their love batteries.

To be sure, we can be cranky and irritable, hard to please and a touch self-centered at times. But to a good human who treats us right we'll give—whenever we can—all our love.

It's a strange symbiosis we've forged over the years, but a positive one for all concerned. Two legs or four, big and bald or small and furry, we've learned to get along, and by doing so we represent a model of what life could be like for everyone. The world could do worse than learn from us.

Though of different persuasions, with different tastes and needs, we live together and it works.